MARKO POGAČAR

→NEON SOUTH

Sandorf Passage books are available to the
trade through Independent Publishers Group:
ipgbook.com | (800) 888-4741.

Library of Congress Control Number:
2021952115

ISBN: 978-9-53351-373-7

This book is published with financial support by
the Republic of Croatia's Ministry of Culture and Media.

MARKO POGAČAR

→NEON SOUTH

TRANSLATED BY
MIRZA PURIĆ

SAN-
DORF
PAS-
SAGE

SOUTH PORTLAND | MAINE

Contents

Every person in this book is an actual person.
Any resemblance to actual persons, living or dead, is purely
coincidental.

The Nude Bolívar

Seven Secretaries of Death

JANIS WAS NAMED for Janis Joplin. To this day, her father plays blues gigs every weekend in bars in the districts of Las Mercedes and La Castellana, where one can still find the odd foreigner, some pudgy gringo, drunk and crazy. During the week he works at the electrical cable factory, and when he comes home, after two hours of breaking through the traffic on out-of-the-way suburban roads, he's too tired: his fingers cramp so badly he doesn't even think about the guitar. As a teenager, Janis used to sing backing vocals, till the ship keeled so much that everything started sliding off the deck, including young girls. She was grounded, and that was the end of her stint with Los Caimanes Voladores. Her home, to be fair, wasn't much safer. The family lives in Petare, one of the world's largest slums, with the population of a smallish European country. In a manner of speaking, they belong to the elite of the district, that solid scab of brick, sheet metal, and plastic sheeting that encrusts the city's knee. Elite—as in prostitution, restaurants, or death squads—means that at least one member of the family is gainfully employed, the lights are on (when there's no power outage), they have clean water in the house (when it decides to come back on), and Janis studies at a public university. We met a thousand words ago, in a blind spot of language; I was in the Americas for the first time, and I wondered if that much was obvious.

Life in Caracas is turning into a nightmare, faster every day, she writes. And it's hard for Europeans to imagine a nightmare in the tropics. The average temperature is 22°C year-round, palm and mango trees stroke the stuffy air, the smell of hot salsa and arepas spreads from the gardens of small bars and somewhere high up, parrots hold council. This is where the film is interrupted, the roll runs out, and the machine spins on and on, clicking away emptily. All that remains of the oil-fueled prosperity of the 1950s and '60s is the memories of those old enough to remember, distant, wizened dotards terrified by the emptiness of the pharmacy shelves. The golden era of Chavismo, when I met both Janis and the city, is also a thing of the past. Although the oil-based economy was thoroughly abused and ill conceived, the downtrodden, disenfranchised majority have certainly benefited tangibly from it. Still, the revolution, in many ways akin to the Yugoslav one, thaws away, cracked at by interventionism and domestic reaction. Today, Caracas is the most dangerous city on the planet not engulfed in war, with a murder rate not much lower than that in Mogadishu. Considerate corpses turn to stone; curmudgeonly ones rot away tirelessly. Life is a burglarized kiosk. Crocodiles have come, bitten, and locked their jaws, like flying caimans from a fairy tale that hijack your dream and you can't fall asleep anymore.

On the grass of Parque del Este, we devour those terrifying, Gulliverian hot dogs, oversized like everything else in this cramped, restless world. The vendor, working off the back of his bike cart, piles up pickles, fried onions, lettuce, mustard, and tears, so high on top of them that franks and buns can only be accessed in a deductive fashion. It's early beer season. Local reggae music smolders in the air; Janis knows the lyrics and hums along between bites. She talks about the sloth. It must've been ten years since her father found him, stunned, at the end of a row of houses. A car had probably hit him. They nursed him for months, that half-blind, foul-smelling animal, till he was able to hang upside down unaided from the satellite dish mounting pole. When they carried him back to the jungle, a pack of children cried themselves into spasms, as if walking behind a coffin. His praises were sung in a slow, minor-key song by Los Caimanes Voladores. Like the sloth, the song was called "Juanito."

* * *

His name remains lost in the black volcanic sand. There are probably no prospectors searching for gold nuggets of memory who would be able to pan it now from the heaving waters of Laguna de Apoyo. The rest, however, I remember well, because the overripe mango that briefly froze in the air like a world shorn of time did not land on my head after all.

As a child, I believed that ornithology was a truncated, human-friendly version of otorhinolaryngology, a branch of medicine I encountered regularly at the time. Birds? Their only purpose was to be caged, shot at from slingshots, rumored to be lassoed for dinner by this or that neighbor as the story may require, or caught, slyly, craftily, by coating a branch with glue. Thus trapped and useless, they were thrown by their vanquisher into those cages again. One whose name I've forgotten made a living as a birder. At least that's the way one might explain it to a child. He was unable, he said, to take his eyes off them. To him, the sky wasn't a blue sheet of emptiness, but an uninterrupted, round-the-clock symphony of hummingbirds, toucans, house swallows, and resplendent quetzals, a regular evening session of a parrot assembly, and an endless palette of plumage, as motley and colorful as a naive painter's dream. Now in his thirties, he grew up in Granada, one of the oldest cities in Central America, some 30 kilometers away. The difference between Managua, home to the institute of ornithology, and Granada, home to his family, the place from which he climbs up here to his permanent exploration post in the eye of the extinct volcano, is a creaky, rotting-from-the-inside-out metaphor of the difference between the "old" and the "new" world. On Saturday, December 23,

1972, at 12:29 local time, the capital was hit by an earthquake, never to recover completely. Managua today looks like a bag of Monopoly houses strewn randomly all over the jungle, with the odd hotel, bank, or shopping mall stretching skyward. Granada, tucked between the mass of the still-active Mombacho and Lake Nicaragua, has retained its colonial architecture. These two views are nothing but two faces of the same exploitation project whose machetes cut into the gold, the coffee, and the tobacco as much as they cut into the flesh itself. The former doesn't try to hide the punishment meted out by the evil white god. The latter, reminiscent of a death mask, has been spruced up in a series of botched cosmetic surgeries.

We chase beers with sugar cane aguardientes, distilled at home by his father. Bird-watching, unfortunately, can be tedious, especially when there aren't any exciting birds to watch, or when they fall asleep, go extinct, or simply don't show up. Passions gradually melt away, even more so when they grow into a job. His father was a Sandinista guerrillero. On the day Somoza was toppled, he unfurled with his own hands the flag of the revolution on the National Assembly. Today, fourteen of them—four generations—live in a house with an open garden and iguanas loitering about. Four children swinging in hammocks are his. Their great-grandfather watches them. Riveted to the stroller, he is suffocating in the smoke of his cheap Casino King Size cigarettes, which he never ceases to blow, like a steam locomotive, the kind that used to bring adventurers into Granada—some of them soaked in madness, like Klaus Kinski in *Fitzcarraldo*—and take them out of the city rich or dead. The most persistent ones stayed, desiccated in the red soil loosened and crushed by mahogany roots into fine, gunpowder-like dust. The relative humidity is extremely high. Carne mechada, enchiladas, and black beans on the table. When he recounts how a rotten mango fruit crashed down on a drunken me somewhere up on the dark lakeside beaches, and I leapt up thinking someone was shooting, the four kids and the grandfather laugh with their toothless mouths. The father, a retired guerrillero, keeps his silence. Night falls on Nicaragua.

* * *

"Are we really cursed?" asks Manolo, squeezing the thick neck of his gun.

"And if so, who is the cosmic bastard who put the curse on us?" he says, although this sounds like a translation of a line from a novel by Enrique Vila-Matas.

"It's possible, after all, if the curse is strong enough, if it's so thoroughgoing that it can split the ground and make one's teeth fall out, it's possible then that we're talking about a benefactor here, about a blessing given without much thought," he says. But his mouth isn't moving; Manolo is completely mum as he squeezes the cold

MARKO POGAČAR

gun barrel, and his soliloquy echoes only in my sweaty head blasted by gusts of wind as cold as the gun. We gaze at Puno, where the line steamboat *Yavari* is at anchor beneath the slopes sprinkled with agave trees and a forest of brick houses, rather than toward the gray offing of Lake Titicaca drowned in thick fog, the offing one had better be silent about.

To me, Manolo is an Indio. From his perspective, of course, the matter looks different. When I ask what that rapier-truncated conquistador word means to him, he shrugs. "Doesn't mean anything. May mean a man. A man who doesn't want to die," says Manolo as he stumbles, tries to catch his balance on the island withes soaked in lake water. He spends most nights over in Puno, with his wife, although it happens now and again that he sleeps here, where he grew up, on this particle of land cobbled together from flotsam, reeds, and wire. Every day except Sunday, he took a motorboat to attend school in town. Every Saturday morning, he traveled half an hour to El Puerto Adventist Church, a house of worship reminiscent of a fire station that the red assault vehicles abandoned and left the community dependent on fire-prevention measures—a divine supervisory authority responsible for raging soul fires.

On the islet, one of the largest among the forty similar small islands making up the Uros archipelago, he sells sandwiches and trinkets to tourists who stop there on their way to the Taquile or Isla del Sol. Sometimes, in front of his mother's wattle house, he conducts a motley choir which, for a few sols, sings hymns in praise of the Savior to those same tourists, in Quechua, a mystical, secret language to me, but not, of course, to the Savior, who is one absolute polyglot of a savior. And hopelessly cute, like people who say "no!" to dogs.

The gun Manolo shifts from one hand to the other is a mere shell of a gun, a skeleton unworthy of a burial. His grandfather put it together half a century ago, hammering a nail into the trigger, whittling down a piece of yellow-painted wood washed ashore into the stock. It was intended for hunting the Atitlán grebe, an animal that looked like it was made up by Josef Švejk to be featured in his zoology magazine. Today it mostly serves for Manolo to squeeze its windpipe with his fish scale-covered fingers as his gaze wanders the long-deteriorated inside of the barrel, a region inhabited even longer by raw darkness.

I ask what god means to him, the one that he still worships every Saturday, rushing across the biggest navigable lake on the continent, the freshwater basin that towers 4,000 meters above the seawater.

"Means nothing. Means a man who refuses to die. It could be that god is one of your Indios," Manolo says with a shrug and a smile.

"Yes, god is an immortal Indio."

* * *

MARKO POGAČAR

It's night above the American cities, the beehives twinkling like a stellar jungle beneath the Southern Cross that glows in the darkness like an incandescent hammer, and is itself nothing but a sum of celestial bodies swaying slightly above the cities, as if someone soft and distant were breathing up there. That someone knows the history of burning flocks. That someone sees a bird as it falls. That unreal someone.

* * *

H. bears the most famous Colombian surname. To this day, most people smell in it blood and arson, its sonic footprint is short bursts of gunfire, its postcards those fleeing hippos driven insane on their retaliatory rampage through the calles and carreras of Medellín. But, for the inhabitants of the poorest barrios that tumble down the hillsides like an avalanche of Lego pieces, it sounds close, homely, perhaps fatherly. Often they call him *Hermano; El Presidente,* they whisper. H. never had to live the reality of the poor neighborhoods, the everyday life of most of her fellow citizens. Until her twenties, she'd only seen slums through tinted car windows. She met her relative just a few times. She had turned ten the week he was fatally shot, and Medellín, adorned with a bloody sash, triumphantly took the title of the world's murder capital. He gave her a birthday present, a plush, life-size Siberian tiger cub. The beast, somewhat dusty, still purrs, forgotten in the cage that is her room.

Since the hatchets were buried, the situation in the city has calmed down. The cartels and the guerrillas are peaceful now, which means they wage war by other means. Truckloads of mostly foreign money have been pumped into infrastructure, institutions, and community development, with the government only in partial control. Pupils in white uniforms. Overground Metro line, students gushing out of it. Cultural centers festooned with fluttering rainbow flags and lingering Christmas tinsel, sounds of melodrama echoing from the roofs, from the screens as gray as a heart, couples crumpling up in the courtyards. "Guantanamera." José Martí and the us torture facility in the bay where the woman the song is about hails from are equally far from those wise, powerful bodies. Rhythm slides down the drumheads and unplastered facades; like a bullet, it stops and nestles itself in the middle of an inextricable skein of nerves where it grows exuberantly, proliferates like living flesh.

Not far from Botero's *Bird*—a metal sculpture turned into a shrapnel bomb with twenty kilos of explosives that went off during a music festival in 1995, killing thirty and wounding over two hundred, a pile of blossomed steel still standing there in memory of the dead—trade is conducted in the cramped space in the shade of the railway tracks. Rancid life howls from the low stalls and vendor carts: flybespittled tins of dulce de leche, dried armadillos sprawled out on the fresh fruit. More exotic merchandise, merchandise loose and dangerous, hops like circus fleas from pocket to pocket; you can try it, like fresh cheese, off a key or a knife. I need a deodorant to tame the sweat ripening under my shirt. I want those small bananas, to wolf them down as I wait for H. Taunting starts. I don't pay attention; I swallow bananas instead and try to puff up a bit, like a blunthead pufferfish, a fish whose name sounds as though whoever came up with it was fucking around. I'm suddenly happy to be tall and balding, with a fresh haircut; for a second I'm larger than myself, like a balloon with a picture of Reagan on it. However, the enemy hasn't been fooled. A few shady characters get up and head toward the blunthead, now puffed out. I leap to my feet and flee into the crowd.

When I finally meet H. again, it's early, sticky dusk. We get onto the cable car which picks people up from the riverside, where Pablo's misfortunate hippos met their end, and takes them up the slopes, down which runs the glowing city. Below, in the thick pell-mell, in the dark realm of myth, S. and M. follow us on motorcycles. When all four of us meet again on the hilltop, at the city's rim, a spectacle bursts down below. Millions of lights aflicker, as if to compete with the sky, as if there were nothing worth abandoning.

* * *

Don Pablo, they would say.

El Patrón, El Rey, El Mágico, they would say, gazing at the floor or the tips of their shoes; *El Pablito,* begged those who had once been close to him, those who had wronged him somehow, both looking deep into the heart of the earth, lifting their gaze, only to avert it the next moment, burnt by his eyes. Those taller and those shorter than him, those known to him and those unknown alike, they all knew they were speaking for their life.

El Padrino, El Señor, El Zar, they'd say with their heads hung, when he still breathed.
   Swine, they said when he died.

*   *   *

Raymond is a poet. He was born in Chile ten years, give or take a day, after that first, fateful, now unjustly forgotten, dishonored September 11, when a bullet from a Kalashnikov—a gift from Fidel Castro—decided to fall asleep in Allende, and Chile sank into twenty years of dictatorship. His father was a short-story writer who fled from the junta in the mid-'80s following some problems with the secret police, first to Panama, then—as Raymond was entering his teens—Costa Rica, where he finally settled down. Right after that, he died in a bizarre, somewhat cinematic climbing accident. Raymond was named after Carver. The silver lining, he says, was that the old man became a father and snuffed it before he managed to read Bolaño. I'm sure he would've liked him, he says, he would've gone bonkers for crazy Bolaño, even more than for Carver, and my name would've been Roberto. Nothing wrong with that name; on the contrary, my wife's name is Roberta. But, wouldn't that be dumb, Roberto and Roberta, like in an incredible, maniacal children's film? No, it's a good job the old man had me when he did, and not a day later, says Raymond, Roberto manqué.

We're sitting in the bar La Teta Negra, central San José, a bar that, judging by the clientele, could've been called La Tinta Negra or La Tita Negra, but the name it already has suits it best: black tit, with the black milk of daybreak dripping from it, drop by drop, as the night passes. We suck on bottles of Imperial and chase them with pisco, a Peruvian spirit distilled several times over. The better part of the Tit's patrons live by the pen, reporters mostly. Raymond, too, patches up his budget with articles, mainly in the culture section of the English-language paper *The Tico Times*. Fortunately, he still doesn't resemble the duo at the adjacent table, the two veterans steadfastly manning the post: underhaired, overweight, wearing fishing vests and mustaches yellow from cigarette smoke—an unmistakable, hyperrealistic portrait of newsroom lifers, recognizable all over the planet. The chatter on Avenida Central, the street vendors' hawking, the punctured exhausts of motorbikes, the musicians butchering a standard unknown to me, the birds, the thousands of loudspeakers supplying the scene with a dancy atmosphere, all these things withdraw following the metronome of the minute hand. This superhuman bundle of noise, as loose as the smoke, is then transferred inside, to the bars and enclosed beer gardens, along with the people. The city contracts and expands all around, like an anemone or a predatory deep-sea sponge driven insane by the tiny organisms getting stuck in its pores, its folds that are nothing but teeth, fangs. It's as humid as the sea bottom and the tropical night strikes from all sides, a monster of a night, a night larger than itself. Peanut shells crunch underboot; a dull march is playing on the radio. The waiter keeps repeating something I don't understand.

When he has a few drinks, Raymond calls me El Poeta, and I respond in kind, because it sounds nice in Spanish. After a few more drinks, he likes to go on and on about the Latin American essence and the Latin American curse, about the idea of home, homeland, and homelessness as destiny. What am I, he asks? I left my native country when I was two. I started school in Panama, but there's nothing there except that stupid channel. I grew up right here, in Costa Rica. A few thousand kilometers away. Same language. I've left the continent only once: I went to Paris, to see Baudelaire's grave. What am I then, tell me, asks Roberto manqué, focused on a hidden point lost in the grease-stained calendar of the forgotten year 2008. You, Ray, are a poet, and a bit of a fool. A drunken fool, if I may add, shouts the waiter, pushing a CD into the player. His personal Jesus, as vast as guilt, suddenly teeters about the room.

* * *

B. sharpens knives. In his part of Barranco, steep winding steps descend to the ocean, to the beach where life incessantly settles into a sandy crypt, a gray mosaic above which green, surfing, basilisk-like Lazaruses try at once to get up, rise on their fragile boards, and walk on the water, all in one fell, counterbiblical swoop. In the middle of the neighborhood stands the church Ermita de Barranco, also a postcard of life and death at the same time. Not an ordinary mantra about the afterlife, but rather quite tangible an image, an icon metaphorically becoming of the church in general. Its yellow facade with two little steeples and a heavy wooden door, everything that can be seen from the ground, has been refurbished and shines in its luxuriousness. The roof, a barrel-like boat made of wood and adobe under the sky's direct watch, has caved in, broken, dusty and stripped bare, akin to the ribcage of a sun-bleached buffalo. Like priests, stout vultures perch on the beams in their frocks of black plumes. The soundtrack of the scene comprises, along with the hiss of waves and surreally unpleasant incantations of birds, a barely audible but persistent *skh, skh, skh*: the sound of time passing sleeplessly, the sound of a blade pressed against a hard stone.

Now, this is, possibly, hard to believe, but B. sharpens knives, and there's nothing sinister to it. The job he's been doing over the last sixty years involves honing metal dulled with use to a state of exemplary sharpness. How those silent tools come to lose their initial quality is outside of B.'s area of interest. Just like their sharp future, which is at the same time quite certain and wholly uncertain, that piece of information belongs to the sphere of professional discretion. B. has four children. All four were raised on this swarf, says B., as he presses the treadle with his foot. The treadle moves the belt, and the belt spins the wheel, sticky and rough under the fingertips, like a tongue. A ginger cat is lolling about in the circular shadow cast by the spinning grinding wheel. I slurp icy Cristal as the sun's savage signet sears its signature into the asphalt of Ayacucho Street and the sizzling skin of my skull, and I listen to the story of the children of the blade.

Ana, the eldest, was born under General Pérez Godoy's junta, when subversive machetes were furtively sharpened for an extra sol in the darkness of hallways and back gardens. If we consider the average price of tools and cutlery, as well as the Southerners' proverbial thriftiness, we arrive at a thesis about a golden era of grinding, one supported many times over by Ana's childhood. She grew up in a nice house in the district of La Victoria, in a side street domed by acacias and palm trees, and she studied at a public university. She buried her first husband after his car disappeared in the waters of the Urubamba under mysterious circumstances. With her second she runs a real estate agency called Last Respects, with a seat in Arequipa. It's a respectable business indeed: she sells burial plots. Ana has always been B.'s pet.

Her sister Raquel came unexpectedly, more than ten years after Ana. Camila had been with her in their mother's belly the whole time, which B. and his wife learned only when an unexpected foot presented itself to those present at the scene, after the previous two had left the blind sarcophagus that is the mother. Camila has always—possibly because of this—walked with her head in the clouds. Finally, less than a year later, Jorge came into the world as the last child. B. had a habit of seeing the first three children as one, like some six-armed Eastern deity—Kali or, possibly, Vasudhara, B. couldn't say with certainty. All this happened under left-wing general Juan Velasco Alvarado's Revolutionary Government of the Armed Forces. Opportunities for knife sharpeners were shrinking; after all, cheap and durable yet banally ordinary steel from the United States was increasingly available. Suddenly, an air-raid siren resounded somewhere in the sky. My bottle of Cristal toppled and rolled under B.'s feet. The priests darted off the roofs, the cat disappeared in the thicket, Lima's skin crawled. Apparently, a story that never starts is a story that cannot finish.

* * *

A forest is a curious beast. It covers the slopes spread out far below us, just as hair takes a face by surprise and over-grows the topography of that gateway of the throat, where the tongue dips like a subterranean river. Forests are per-sistently burned. They are just as persistently cut down. For-ests are cleared, thinned, and wiped out for coffee to sprout in their place and render man forever sleepless and insane. But no, the conspiracy against the terror of wakefulness has succeeded. Listen: the monkey's ears are ringing. The rustling guerrilla of slumber rises.

*   *   *

Amadeo was not yet ten when they started to address him as maricón, or, at times, marica for short. Word about this matter, rather inconvenient for him at first, went around quickly, Pereira being a small town, at least compared to Bogotá. What Amadeo did back then to earn the less-than-prestigious label was little and nothing: he preferred skipping to shooting strays with a slingshot, felt a bit too passionately about dominoes, and on two occasions, he showed up at the school costume party dressed as a woman. The first time as his own mother, the second as Sister Amorena María Nevia de la Soledad, the catechism instructor from their parish.

Before his teenage years it was all, in every sense, largely innocent. Then he learned what being a marica actually entailed, and accepted the role with open arms. First beatings came. One hot, stuffy monsoon night, he ran into a group of local youths at the Olaya Herrera Park as he was trying to hide in the shadow of the dilapidated railway station, under the balcony that threatened to collapse. Passenger trains in Colombia stopped running when the National Rail Company was liquidated in the mid-'90s, and now the country is dotted with abandoned skeletons of the station network, as needless as the tooth he lost that night. It was harder the second time. Everything happened in the town center; it was barely evening. He was sitting with a group of friends on the plinth of the *Nude Bolívar* at Plaza de Bolívar, a monument as slick and livid as a bruise, as taut as a phallus, as tense as night, the South American night that mounted the whole continent like Simón José Antonio de la Santísima Trinidad Bolívar mounted his icy steed, and slowly descended onto the heads of the beautiful, white-hot Pereira homos. A group of thugs with perfectly clear intentions appeared, armed with brass knuckles and batons, beautiful, hard batons Amadeo would want deep up his ass under different circumstances, and the consequences were just as clearly felt in the morning.

This time his father found out. Amadeo Senior was rather old. He'd been running a bar known as El Rincón Clásico, near Avenida del Río, for over forty years. At the bar, A. Senior (whose real name was actually Mario) incessantly spun classical records on two well-oiled Technics turntables. In addition to the obviously classical music, his selection included classical jazz and tango records, even the odd chanson that only a Frenchman could write (at least back then). At first, Mario was surprised at the news. Then, a few days later, he had a dream of his son, his last child, named for the great, awesome Mozart, in a lavish crinoline from the turn of the century, spinning and spinning to the 3/4 beat of a waltz he was sure was best attributed to Strauss. At that moment the music changes: the dress is now more colorful, his movements faster, more passionate. Mario doesn't hesitate. As the room echoes with the demonic sounds of the divine Piazzolla, he takes his son's hand and spins with ease, switching between lead and follow. Then he startles awake in sweat and calls out: Amadeo, Amadeo, Amadeo, but nobody hears him. He stops shouting, turns on the light, washes his face, goes down to El Rincón and lifts the window bars. That is when I see him.

*　*　*

"I imagined that night as the opening scene from *The Night of the Iguana*," he says.

"Although I'd never seen the film, I imagined that sequence. I saw a huge lizard speeding across the scorched earth. He then stopped for a second, listened, and caught a fly in mid-air with his sticky tongue. It was night for the fly, from that moment on to eternity, which is where the title of the film comes from. Yes, at first I was aware that something was off in terms of logic, but I assumed that iguana, too, would end up under a car tire, or a knife, or a boot. We all end up under something sooner or later, don't we?" he says.

"And then the day came, as days do, like Amadeus in that German song, and that's really how it was, only everything happened even faster, really awfully fast. We were sitting on the monument, this same monument you and I are sitting on now, and the night came cold and hot at the same time, as hot as the blood of all the young gaylords of Pereira, and we were suddenly drenched in our own blood as if in coffee."

"We were terribly awake," he says. "Awake, but at the same time somehow finally asleep. That's all there is to say, really."

A Carnation from a Poet's Grave

The Grandfather

THE GRANDFATHER LANDED in Distrito Federal on a hot, translucent day very early in February, exactly three years after the District's administrative abolishment, and the vast beast of a city melted yet again into a shower of cryotalo and shit known under the name of Mexico City. Of course, it would be more correct to say Ciudad de México, but this undoubtedly more accurate way of putting it would erase from the sentence Kerouac's *Mexico City Blues*, which is nothing the grandfather would know anything, or care one whit, about. He was supposed to be a transit visitor. He would've spent seven hours at the airport with the grandson, drinking coffee and looking at the windows of the souvenir shops, just like that—espresso, souvenirs, and lukewarm tacos, till his midday flight to Havana. The whole affair couldn't have possibly gone smoothly. In an attempt to cross the border, the grandfather was arrested, deprived of documents, and, together with drug mules, migrants, and tattooed, under-age gang members, taken to the squalid airport detention facility. There was a gaping fault line between the two male members of the lineage, namely the death of the country in which they were born, as well as a skein of serpentine state borders sans substance or significance. All this burrowed in the old man's mind like the line from Kerouac's *Mexico City Blues*: "They'll eat your heart alive, Every time," quite certainly, *every time*. It should be noted that the grandfather didn't take it personally. Furthermore, it bears pointing out that the grandfather wasn't *my* grandfather, and that I was by no means concealed behind the code name *grandson*. This crude account, one could claim without compunction, could hardly be considered coded. Regardless of the evident and quite tangible presence of the grandson, the grandfather was no one's but wholly and utterly his own.

Born toward the end of the 1930s, a decade paved with dust and assassinations, at the time of landing he was all of eighty years old, ready to spend the following two decades— to which he felt immutably entitled—making up for two or three tiny omissions in life that he only detected after the fact, something he was, in turn, obliged to do by the equally immutable metronome of death. Since the late '50s, as a student and later a colonel of the Yugoslav Army, the grandfather moved from one republic capital to another, finally settling down—*son, my son, not my son*, endlessly did the cathedral bell ring out those contradictory syllables—at the Naval Command headquarters. Then, in 1985, he came into conflict with the military authorities and was

MARKO POGAČAR

sent into retirement. The war caught him in a village lost on the shady slopes of Mt. Durmitor in Montenegro, in the shadow of his own better past, that impenetrable, treacherous lee of conifers and rotting leaves that hardened commentators have no qualms referring to as youth. Now, at the peak of solitude from which he derived unexpected and still unallocated strength, his bullet was Holy Magnet, the standard operating procedure was replaced by "The Ray of Microcosm," a cosmic epic poem by the prince-bishop Petar Petrović Njegoš. Now, in this soft, deranged twilight filled with nothing but long time and long blood, the grandfather stood at once as the downfall and the triumph of real socialism, its obverse and reverse. Someone who hadn't yet come to terms with the revelation that under the mask of progress hid the boring face of death, before which the future dissolved like the final bars of a nationless national anthem.

He first decided to take a train trip, all the way to the steep streets of Vladivostok, at whose feet slumbered the Pacific Fleet behemoths. Almost immediately after that he set out—this time accompanied by the grandson and a few friends, including myself—along the feather-light tracks of utopia. Dressed in a pair of khaki pants and a deep-blue T-shirt emblazoned with *Jugopetrol Podgorica*, by the grace of the Mexican border police, early in February, he arrived safely in Havana.

Immediately after he landed, that is, after he made himself relatively comfortable at a spacious casa particular at the edge of the district of Vedado, a period of hunger started for the grandfather. The host, a Leningrad-schooled mechanical engineer, spoke fluent Russian and some English, but apart from old-fashioned and possibly too ceremonial introductions, the grandfather was able to remember only the word хорошо, which he repeated obediently. Accustomed to a diet of cheese, yogurt, and home-cooked lamb, like a gray-haired wraith he roamed the streets at the foot of the hotel Habana Libre—that giant TV screen of a building wrapped up less than a year before the revolution, still showing the quite abstract melodrama of Amelia Peláez's mosaics—finally to find, on day three, a dairy in the heart of Old Havana where he supplied himself with a 2.5-kilo block of ripened cheese and a 5-liter jerrican of yogurt, determined never again to leave anything to chance. A girl tapped obscenities in Morse code with her heels on the pavement of Avenida Paseo. American spies dozed off under the visors of their hats. Crosswords lay on the table, solved, forgotten, forlorn.

The following days he spent mainly—*hi-jo, hi-jo, mi hi-jo*, always the same sleepless yo-yo hawked by the street fruit vendor—walking the calles of El Centro, swaggering in front of the schoolgirls sitting on retaining walls in Malecón, or engrossed in the union of fresh and salty water in the delta of Río Almendares, taking swigs of yogurt from a makeshift drinking flask and voicing his approval while identifying cars that were passing by as if an invisible, omnipotent hand inexplicably partial to him were bringing them out straight from the catalog of his own adolescent dreams. There were Prohibition-era Ford pickups powered by Chinese tractor engines, patched-up Chevrolets from the '40s, polished Buicks from the '50s—a Roadmaster Riviera, a Century Caballero, and a turquoise-white Le Sabre—as well as surreal, airborne, DIY-shop-overhauled Cadillacs full of pudgy tourists. Then the motor pool dissolved all over his dotage, vrooming in the cracked exhaust pipes of the Moskvitches, Škodas, and yellow LADAS, finally to solidify into a blind spot of a livid-blue Zastava 125 PZ identical to the one that the grandfather—*son, my son, not my son*, clattered the merciless pistons—had driven to the Podgorica Airport.

When, on a packed one-peso bus that stuttered along La Línea in the direction of Mirador, almost all his savings were picked out of his pocket, the grandfather said, *Doesn't matter how much money you've got, all things happen without any impact, now*. When, two weeks later in a fishing village not far from Playa Girón, where he'd withdrawn to fish, save money, and heal wounds, a rusty hook went through his finger, the grandfather said, *The only cure for morphine poisoning is a bit more morphine*. When he climbed on the plinth of a monument in Santa Clara showing an immense bronze Che squeezing his short carbine, marching ever onward defying death and the laws of physics, the grandfather raised his clenched fists, like Tommie Smith and John

Carlos fused into a single Black body after their victory in 1968, and said, *Let us descend into the grave.*

Down in the crypt with the names of the fallen revolutionaries, a star of daylight fell on the plaque behind which burned dust transported from Bolivia. The grandfather lay a carnation below the bones, wiped his forehead with his sleeve, clenched his fists once again for his own sake, and said, *My son . . . fuck their fucking fathers.*

Jamila Speaks

IT WAS LIKE happiness I can't remember. As if I'd briefly
found myself in a web of wet, sticky light whose rays lifted
me gently off the ground and rocked me like Mother's hand,
like the eye of a lighthouse gazing through the neighborhoods planted thickly between me and the sea during long,
blood-thick nights, nights which, by some miracle, ended
every time, usually just an hour or two after I'd shut the
heavy turquoise shutters to seal off from the daylight the
window through which I observed the slumbering city, the
sow dismembered every night with a light cleaver in an act of
filigree-precision butchery that the dawn put a stop to with
a solar flash flood, the scorching, mindless bomb of the sun.
Sun my mother, *Sun* my father, both doctors, he a lung
specialist, she specializing in kids, Father and Mother—*Sun,
Jamila, Sun*—first in some dirty jungle war, maybe Angola,
possibly Mozambique, I don't know, amongst the fat, never-
changing flies, worms, and bloated bellies, amongst the
spilled intestines in the wet heroic age, before my time; later,

later the Egyptian blue, sphinxes and beautiful noses, mad-ams and comrades, the Non-Aligned Movement, hookah bars, Egypt . . . that's where the name comes from, those six syllables that—*Jamila Medina come here, Jamila Medina shut up*—I'd always had to explain, over and over again—*Egypt, you know, Arabs, mud*—the name that Father and Mother only ever uttered in full with the burden of an imperative, only ever dunked into things that wanted verbs, tearing up along the seams the silence of Holguín, a curmudgeonly city, a city that was flaking away like the livid-blue blinds and didn't like verbs at all.

And now Mother is the one who needs a doctor. Her col-leagues say—*Jamila . . .*—Mother—*says nothing*—colleagues say—*something like that . . .*—Mother fixes her shirt collar, smooths down the wrinkles on her dress with her palm, Mother—*says nothing, this is me speaking for Mother now, as if the voice were coming from her belly, from a forest as deep as an echo*—I hear her colleagues in the hospital corridor, in the halls of the clinic that bears his name—*I never met him, my friend did, on several occasions, he was a dermatologist, like her, a young dermatologist, and Buenos Aires rang so cold, so distant. He specialized in lepers, like the Messiah that he was, a beautiful young Messiah, a guide I'd never met, but I did see him from a distance two or three times; each time it was as though I could reach out and touch him*—I hear her colleagues whis-pering—*He was in fact a poet, an accursed poet of the revolu-tion*—they say, and the wind outside rubs dust against his cheek, his face greater than fear, as great as youth, yes, as great as life itself.

The life buzzing around me, radiating from ten thousand sooty eyes, from the eyes of the dogs that bark especially loudly when a coche americano full of murderers and parasites zooms past, slices through the stuffy air like a lighthouse beam, like a huge ceiling fan, it pulses but I don't hear it, it writhes but I don't see it, the life tucked into a pair of pants, like a four-year-old's. I retreat before it—before Mother's colleagues who tell me, sotto voce, things I don't want to hear, from whose mouths spiders emerge and weave a fragile veil of rumor, before the sellers who shout *morena* as I walk past, before the parrots and salsa dancers and the line for the vanilla ice cream in front of a domed Coppelia— before this thirsting life I retreat into a small apartment on 25th Street, not far from the University Stairs, a box with turquoise blinds, with oily paint flaking off like fish scales, which I bought with the money from a big literary prize named after a poet I love, whose window looks out onto the offing, and before the offing the Malecón slithering like a stiff, scared sand snake. I ascend as the sun—*Sun, Jamila, Sun*—slowly sets. I leap up the stairs, between the pots of ficus and blooming flowers, red-and-white cones gaping like the mouths of animals, stealthing so as to not attract the attention of the tenants' representative whose door is always open, who—*Jamila, Sun*—pokes his nose everywhere. I climb up the spiral of the lighthouse to the murmur of the neighbors, into the aroma of beans and meat, into the sounds of dominoes and arguments and songs about illicit love, past the third-floor apartment in which, so it says right on the plaque, Fidel and Raúl lived during their studies at the same university where I became—*dottoressa, Jamila, Sun*—a doctor of letters, of literature that keeps me alive by flowing like an uncontrollable stream of poetry through things, all things. So I climb up to the door of my apartment, my gait firm, as if it were the last thing I'll ever do.

I open the door and lay the file on the table, a folder with diagnoses in Latin as fake as those who make them; I remove books from the shelf—Luis Cernuda's and Nicolás Guillén's poems (the latter in luxury binding, a special edition to mark the occasion of his winning the thirty-fourth Stalin Peace Prize, original, landed into my mother's hands a long time ago), both novels by Lezama Lima, of which *Paradiso*, particularly *Paradiso*, hits like a sledgehammer in a hot Cuban night, then translations of Calvert Casey—I remove everything that gets in my way before the solar bomb finally sets and I let in the icy beam of the lighthouse, I sit, shaking off magic spells, shaking off gossip from the corridor, insinuations, rumors—*carc, Jamila Sun, carc, Jamila Sun, carc . . . and something else that is tight and incomprehensible, something I won't say, the insipid dregs, the pond scum of a withering language*—I sit, and the shiny blank page barely allows me to make out what for years I believed I was seeing, certain nonetheless, absolutely convinced that it had to come: a guillotine shinier than the glowing sun sliding down toward a neck; the head rolling till it's stopped by a boot. And so I sat behind the turquoise blinds, whistling through my teeth a song by Víctor Jara, the accursed Chilean, I whistled in the dark hissing like gas in the pipes, like a tame snake waiting for death to compress us, to sift us down to nonexistence in its vast sieve, but no, death never came.

I spat on the paper, I pushed the dissipating wood, I wished I could see on it, instead of spittle, if only for a moment, like a prophecy and judgment, the words: *Open the eyes, open the ribs—raise high the veal heart, butchers.*

The Son-in-Law

HE APPEARED SUDDENLY, like a disease or a friend who has
long since stopped bothering to ring the bell, on the grassy
median strip which, like a scalpel sliding down the spinal
cord, like a plow, like a swimmer, evenly split Avenida de
los Presidentes, about halfway between the monument to
general José Miguel Gómez and St. Salvador Allende, as we
were sitting on a bench drinking tepid Cristal. The bench
looked liked the ones strewn across the parks of our childhood stuck into the ground, the good old wooden socialist
bench, the kind that could still be found all over the Socialist Federal Republic of Yugoslavia, much more comfortable
than the metal crap in Paris or the snobby seats of New York
and New England bus shelters. It was Saturday, three in the
morning; the strip was packed with tipsy minglers corralled
there into the no-man's land by the municipal police, who
took their time, only blowing their whistles here and there
as they cleared Malecón. As the cafeterias and discos and
even the bars of bad death closed, and as tribute concerts for

the victims of last week's hurricane—the winds that were apparently following me—finished one by one, the throng around the benches swelled; hot rum evaporated through the skins, intoxicating moths and bats, wiping seagulls and collared doves off the sky on its march through the ether as both a wave and a particle, akin to slow, very slow, liquid buckshot.

The last bar de mala muerte we left in a full lineup of four drunken freaks sticky with the night, stuttering after the thread of seeping street light we tried to follow. Along the way we were kicking hairy mango stones and blowing kisses to the busts of José Martí, the gypsum wraiths scattered around the gardens and quiet porticos. From our feet also evaporated an irresolute, reluctant, and hesitant embarrassment of movement, the unbearable stiffness of human trees that barely muster up the courage to sway in the hot gale of salsa, and the flesh gradually forgot the betrayal of fraternal flesh, the body the allure of the bodies in the beat. As soon as we reached Vedado, J. collapsed on his bed, and fifteen minutes later three men approached our bench, headed by a skinny dude whose eyes told tales. The biggest of the three, a Black man who reminded one of a molting Mr. T, had a boom box under his arm blasting Queen's "Innuendo." They walked up to us and asked if we'd share some beer. When we gave them our cans, they took a swig each, weighed the cans in their hands, and took off running with them, clumsily, as if in a slapstick piece or an opera buffa. *Hey, man! Can't do that! Get back here with those beers!* I shouted in the language of the South Slavs as a faraway Ritchie Blackmore squealed from the loudspeakers. This is where the sketch is interrupted, expectedly and unexpectedly at the same time; the melody stopped in midair, as stiff as a terrified rabbit, and the skinny guy in a cap emblazoned with *Pedro* sat by me and started to talk. At first his words were knotty, almost unintelligible; they came rolling in like a slow avalanche of syllables over the dike of the throat and time, as if picked out of the cold ashes of oblivion with a fire iron. "I non-'ligned, I non-'ligned" was the message that was reaching me with a delay of ten or more years, and the scrawny fellow was becoming more articulate with every sentence, more and more intelligible, till the words finally started to do what words do: flow unstoppably and meld into the thick magic of speech.

"You know Bata Životinja? Bata the Animal? He dieded," he said, and in my memory an almost withered May night in Belgrade opened up like a rose of Jericho. The pavement in Zdravko Čelar Street burst into bloom, the asphalt the news of the passing of one of Yugoslavia's biggest film stars bounced off, announced by the newscaster's throaty voice that came through the open window from an apartment lit only by a TV screen. Then I remembered J.'s story about officers of the Polisario Front who'd studied in Yugoslavia and were now stationed at camps in the Algerian desert.

The first thing they wanted to know, after more than thirty years of absence: Does Lepa Brena still sing?

The sky over Havana was rent by an orange scream, lost like a telegram between two worlds, a still unsigned pact of two nights, a cry that could have come from one of the haunted rooms of Edíficio Palace, a former hotel, or from anywhere in the direction of Avenida Paseo.

"He died, yes. A few years ago," I squeezed through my teeth, like a drowsy prophet.

"Dieded, I know, Bata call on telephone and said, 'I am going to died.' And really," he said, "then he dieded."

The skinny Marcos with *Pedro* across his forehead was neither an insane spiritual medium nor a liar or a drug addict in the strict sense: Marcos with eyes that bore witness, who was already speaking fast and fluently and sweating under his cap, was Bata's son-in-law, when he was a student from a nonaligned country. "Belgrade, after war, nineties, crazy people, bombing, booom, everything burn, café, Belgrade nice, piglets, mechanical engineering, you know the pillar on that hill, Avalon." He married Helena, Bata's granddaughter, and they had a son, Andrej, a beautiful little Mongoloid whose condition, along with "a little bit drinking, little bit craziness, and Belgrade women, and North, such big North, city so gray only white when snow," wedged itself between them, sending him finally back into the wound of a dense Havana night. Bata came to visit twice, they "drinked rum, smoked cigara, went to Cine Yara"—and left him "money for all year," but Marcos never went to Belgrade again; he never saw Andrej again since he'd left, he never heard Helena's voice.

The silence from the body of the receiver, the silence from the few-and-far-between letters, the silence of a lost language that rings out in the chatter of voices and the noise of whistles, the odd shout and "Speed King" from powerful speakers; of a slick language that left Mr. T and the third fellow amazed, like a possessed housewife delirious in fluent Latin; of a language that was alive to me, but to Marcos it was near dead, that silence briefly fell between us, connecting us in a surreal way, stretched like a shame-and-death-flavored chewing gum, embodied in a translucent yet impenetrable bubble of defeat. We emptied the cans of Cristal and a bottle of Havana Club. Spirits hovered freely now, the memory roses of Jericho opened up like alveoli, like a mutated family tree over which circled specters of seagulls, and on its branches, the hanged gently swayed in the wind. We shook hands and followed the silhouettes of the dark torsos till they disappeared in the direction of Calle Zapata, as the night thinned out, and quieter and quieter became the drunks, and the smell of the nightmarish sea flooded the nostrils, rising in its blind contempt for the forces of the earth as only the lecherous musk of the sea could.

Then the dawn broke and sleep came as a sentence after which no one would ever again tremble with fear of the possibility that there may be such a thing as pardon, and that someday he might actually be released.

Kike

THE ROAD TO SANTA CLARA. A 1956 Chevrolet Bel Air,
turquoise-white, with one love, one madness, and some
despair compacted under the celestial dome of the hood,
powered by the furious beating of a transplanted trac
tor heart, that galleon at once separated from the world
and faithfully bound up with it tore up the asphalt at a
speed of 120 kilometers an hour, planting in me the seed
of a southern, melancholy happiness. The sun reflected
on the chrome plated rearview mirror, grazed the windows of the sugar refinery, and stopped on the panels
which in lieu of Coca-Cola and Telecom ads bore inscrip-
tions such as: *More socialism, more freedom, more solidarity*
or *Onward to a revolutionary future*. Hot wind lashed the
black beat of the continent out of the ears: over the rat-
tlesnake death rattle of shakers and snare drums, over
the liquid sound of the organ, the Lizard King screamed
out his own obituary:

Blood in the streets in the town of New Haven
Blood stains the roofs and the palm trees of Venice
Blood in my love in the terrible summer
Bloody red sun of fantastic L.A.

and at the town entrance, in the middle of the incandescent belt of the roadway, four vultures were ripping up a carcass of unknown origins. I lowered the window greased up by flies and breathed in the smell of feathers and death, a night terror of light and dust, freedom's cloying signature.

Enrico Mariano Gagualera, aka Kike, a Calabrian on his mother's side—second-generation Caribbean; his mother's mother was still kneading macaroni and cursing with gusto in some village not far from Cosenza—was sitting with his cap back to front, and, with a cone made out of a copy of the *Granma*, the official organ of the Communist Party of Cuba, on his bare ankle he was drumming a beat viciously similar to the throb of a galley drum. The *Granma* was named after the yacht from which the revolutionaries—eighty-two of them—led by the future comandantes Fidel, Raúl, Che, and Camilo, landed here in 1956, with barely twenty of them making it to the jungle of Sierra Maestra, which in turn, almost two years later, resulted in the hijacking of an armored train and Batista's final defeat right here on the streets of Santa Clara. Around him, Parque Leoncio Vidal was pulsing with the sighs of a February afternoon. Pensioners were orbiting around the square in smaller and smaller circles, children were paying a peso each for a ride on a little train harnessed to a goat, bells were ringing and pigeons cooing, pecking at something akin to souls.

Enrico Mariano Gagualera, aka Kike, was named for his father, Enrique, an RTO trained first in the USSR, then by North Vietnamese instructors, who left his bones in some god-forsaken corner not far from Luanda in the winter of 1976, on the edge of the rain forest sprawling from the coastline all the way to the resplendent, cyclopic blind spot of all of Africa, a spot resembling a large drop of blood. When the news arrived via the telegraph to Santa Clara, his mother had already been screaming with considerable intensity because Enrique's lacerated, still unnamed head was emerging from between her legs. Perhaps that, too, that furious collision of the bare crown of his head and the death announcement that impressed itself into his flesh like a bite of destiny, he says, is the reason why he has remained loyal to the Cuban cause his whole life, but also a convinced anarchist, a reader of Mikhail Bakunin and the accursed Errico Malatesta. Kike speaks fluent Italian, French, and English. He starts the conversation with "Do you by any chance speak Czech?" He knows more about World War II in Yugoslavia and the Wars of Yugoslav Succession than an average Zagreb student. He leafs through the economic indicators of Cuba, possibly somewhat doctored, as if through the Central Committee Yearbook: either he really is a student exchange officer at the local university—*with several hundred foreign students, as many as four Americans*—or he is on the payroll of the Dirección de Inteligencia. The two are, after all, not mutually exclusive.

We head to El Mejunje with Kike. The club rose on the ruins of an abandoned colonial-era hotel. It's a café by day, while at night the open garden is flooded with quivering, rhythm-crazed molasses of local scenesters, gays, lesbians, transsexuals under heavy, sweat-smudged makeup, pot-heads, and old punks. A group of his friends appears, rum is flowing, more rum, and blinding cocktails; bats shake the crown of a regal black locust tree, and medical students dance with delighted maricas.

"The evening started like any other," he says, "the evening when it was announced Fidel had died." He was at a punk rock show, drunk on the night and the West, when two policemen interrupted the band that was playing like there's no tomorrow. First they just flailed their arms as if they'd gone insane or got caught by the mad mosh-pit machine, then one of them managed to get his hands on the microphone and shout over the deafening drums: ¡El comandante está muerto! At first it may have sounded like a provocation or a chorus, but it was nothing of the kind; it was sheer truth. The place went silent instantly; there was, after all, a tomorrow, but at the same time it was as if there wasn't, as if that which had arrived with the sun were at the same time ordinary and had a parched throat, as it happens on a hungover morning, and in some strange way devoid of light, separated from what was to come by adding itself up into the soundless abyss of the future. A national week of mourning was declared, and the cold ashes were driven around Cuba for a week, just like Tito's were driven around Yugoslavia, until they found peace under a plaque with his name nailed to a living rock resembling a millstone, down in Santiago. As he tells the story, Kike starts to cry, fixes his gaze briefly to the floor littered with beer caps and cigarette butts, then wipes his face with his shirt.

The next day, it's down the road to Cienfuegos, a seaside town built by French refugees after the Louisiana Purchase. The train timetable Kike doodled on a scrap of paper is invalid; the line has been discontinued for months. "The question is if it ever will," says the clerk with awfully thick glasses, glasses in which I make out the reflection of some boys dragging a fluffy dog around the platform, a vendor of vegetables, nibbles, and newspapers, short passenger cars crowding the greasy tracks, an engine just about to announce departure with a whistle, myself, dark faced and fat from delayed death, all the birds in the sky above us, and the squares of Santa Clara as they evaporate and blend with the sky to form an empty theater; as if a prolepsis, I see in the glass a fish cramped into a tank its own length, something between a pike and a sturgeon, a predatory fish, possibly from a far-flung shithole in Siberia, which stalks the finger all the time and bites at the first opportunity—the saddest, most melancholy fish I'd ever seen. Like a breath of the past and the reflection of something from the future, a hot star of light flashed in the corner, a sun that descended underground to be the match to light the candle, set ablaze the crypt like a stack of hay in a womb, so that the accursed poets of the revolution rise, so that the word becomes the bread and the bullet.

Hemingway Speaks

SHORT SENTENCES, of course. Short, Martha, like volleys of gunfire for someone respected; like the breath of a man running, or a thought of death in the moment when one can already smell the bull.

It's high time you were on your way. The house has been paid for; I gave the Frenchman $12,500, almost the entire down payment, and I've had the key since yesterday. It's called Finca Vigía and lives up to the name. Havana below it steams in the afternoon mist like a cup of tea; the dome of El Capitolio gleams, and it's almost impossible not to hear the sound of the bells. From the back veranda the eye glides across the thick stand of palms and mango trees, down onto the muddy suburbs and the palaces of the pale-faced gentry, and farther along the thread of the road hits the ramparts of the city, which seems so innocent from here, as if just born, like in Lezama Lima's poem. Farther, beyond the forest of flesh and concrete, beyond the mill of the salsa, a dance that certainly contains something mystical, possibly something prayerful, an unreal sheet of blue stretches all the way to Miami. Somewhere halfway between, I seem to be able to make out the chimney of a house in Key West, and I think cormorants are taking off from it. If you would bring a pair of high-magnification military binoculars to your eyes, you could see, I swear, Martha, on the waves woken by the afternoon wind, Pilar swaying serenely like dancers' sweaty thighs. On that porch I sit waiting for your decision, a confirmation that takes nothing more than a postcard, three simple letters in Morse code. Do not write letters. Words should not be wasted. Parrots screech insufferably, hammering is heard somewhere, Europe is a bubbling cauldron, and it's only a matter of time before the world boils over again. Read Catalonia as a prologue; this is where the story actually starts. Save your commas, Martha; they are the desperate sighs of the text, and be wary of the full stop. When the trenches are dug up again, words will come like steel needles to suture the wounds. In the meantime, I add another cube of ice and wait, as dark suffocates this sold-off stand of palms and my dismembered sleep, and Cuba totters off home on rickety legs, and collapses into the darkness like a woman with a heavy, restless dagger of rum prickling her chest.

I woke up hungover. On the table in the spacious, almost-empty canteen, the room into which I intend to move the library, I found an impetuous typed letter to Martha, crumpled up and somewhat wet. It abounded with phrases, beamed with excessive sweetness, and, buttressed with the odd verse by one of the Cuban poets I'd been reading, it depicted me as unacceptably weak. If I'd been Martha, I would've probably asked myself if that was the same giant of a man whom I'd looked in the eye three times and said *I do* to a few months prior, and I would've let the loser wait, just let him wait in that resplendent jungle henhouse, surrounded by monkeys. I ripped it up, rolled a clean white sheet into the carriage of my Underwood, and started this island diary.

Finca Vigía is the jackpot: Martha was right, it would seem. (*Say it precisely like this on the phone!*) All alone as I am here, with bare walls and only the indispensable servants, equipped with my shotgun, an armful of shirts, and hardly any books, I sense the inexplicable thickness of time that is gushing forth. That time roars in me like an earthquake in my middle ear, as if all the roulettes of all the casinos of El Centro were ripped out of the tables and rolled down the street unstoppably, crushing everything in their path—people, cars, dreams—dancing a wild foxtrot under the crystal dome of Tropicana, while the drummer and the brass section of Alfredo Brito's orchestra keep a thunderous drum roll with fanfares going, seemingly forever. True, the pool is smaller than the one Pauline had built in Key West, but there is a tennis court at the property, a red desert I will personally plow up as soon as the first rackets arrive. (*Have Luis order four pairs of Super Winner Deluxe, pronto!*) For a moment, although it makes no sense, it seems to me that it is a little empty and quiet here, after all. Everything around me, every eye and every bush and every hinge actually hisses and roars, and then I realize I miss the cats. More than anything else, I miss the cats.

Fourth morning in the house. I have claimed the wildest among the beasts Luis was feeding with chicken heads on the driveway. A dark stripe runs down her spine, melting over the cataracts of the rib cage, like an eclipse possibly somewhat lengthier but by no means final, and it is with a degree of disappointment that I report here that she possesses a full complement of five toes. I called her Princessa, and she's found her place on a table, which henceforth I shall consider a desk. And I actually sat at the typewriter intending to shorthand last night's dream: a night terror which, it seems to me, could become the kernel of a story.

It was one of those plots that start at some point, only to continue—after a sharp cut, without an explanation or any appreciable logic behind this—at a completely different, possibly quite distant point. The first scenes took place here, but not in the house. I was lying on my stomach on a metal bed in a room in the Hotel Ambos Mundos, and in my dream it was as if I'd just woken up from a terrifying dream. The fan, which I hadn't noticed before, was slicing the stale, smoke-addled air, and on each side of my pillow stood Pilar and Martha, like wraith nurses, or simply two succubi. Suddenly, this serene and at the same time unbearably rough picture is interrupted. I am on a field hospital bed, surrounded by a multitude of such beds. Pilar and Martha

MARKO POGAČAR

are no longer in my sight, and I don't have the slightest idea as to where I am. However, I somehow know it's neither Spain nor Italy, although I seem to be in Europe again. My boots and neatly folded pants by the wall of the tent suggest that it's probably a military hospital and that I was wearing a uniform when I was admitted. There are fans in the room again, spinning clusters of bottle-green meat-market flies into vortices. The murmur amplifies till it reaches an unbearable volume; I'm drenched in sweat, freezing and my shirt billows up as if my heart swelled up multiple times its size just before it burst. A white six-toed cat hops out of my shirt and meows, and I know I've finally died. Snow White is still squatting on my chest and meowing, disconsolate, as if nothing in the whole world could replace me tonight. She cuddles for a while, then becomes upset in an instant: she pisses into my wide-open eyes.

The Grandson

I SAT WITH the grandson in the garden of a restaurant in the
City of a Hundred Fires and ate the worst pizza I'd had in a
long while, an underbaked glob of slop that looked amazingly
like my mother's wartime pizzas. Prado Street was badly illuminated; it seemed as though it hadn't been lit by anything
serious in a while, not a single bonfire, possibly the odd light-
bulb in the sockets on the ceilings of spacious entrances, and
a single candle, lonely in front of a bronze figurine of Benny
Moré, the undisputed king of guaracha. That soft, refined
darkness, however, stood in stark contrast with the fanfare of
the gloaming, the shiny trumpet that until a moment ago was
roaring in a long forte, a seemingly undeletable explosion of
sound and color, and—like a background tattooed into the
retina of the beholder—it added to the inconspicuous ele-
gance of Prado. We finished our pizza and got up, ordered
two Cristals to take away, and as we waited for the beer to
arrive, we watched the scissors flashing in the barbershop
with a framed picture of Comandante Camilo nailed above

the mirror, while the movable neck of the chair, rotating barely noticeably, diligently gathered the clipped hair that turned it into the fourth bearded Comandante.

The moment we stepped onto the pavement of Prado, Unamuno was behind our back. At first he was like a shadow, a stain like those that bloat up the plastering for years before they finally swallow the entire surface, or like a parable of conscience from a children's illustrated history of psychoanalysis. A shadow, after all, prompted us to turn around in the first place. The light of the few street lamps suddenly stitched up an inexplicable, playful excess of limbs to our slim torsos, as if an octopus had been tailing us, or Goddess Kali. Unamuno was a tall, broad-shouldered Black man, well in his sixties; he wore a cocked baseball cap and incessantly hopped and skipped in a low guard. "No fear!" he shouted. "I don't hit. Just an old tic," he added, now gasping a little bit.

He was part of the Olympic Team in Moscow in 1980, when the fridges and store windows of the socialist world were invaded and occupied by the games' mascot, the silly bear Misha. Teófilo Stevenson won his third Olympic heavyweight gold and inscribed himself forever in the history of boxing, and in the hearts of eight million Cubans, while Unamuno, twenty-eight at the time, discovered in himself a previously deeply buried love of philosophy.

It happened at a dinner in the run-up to the final bout. Unamuno (whose real name was Miguel Yuniel) was sitting between Raúl, recently retired, a little cross-eyed secretary of the Cuban Boxing Federation, and a young lady from Spain he didn't know—a gorgeous Catalonian or Basque, Unamuno couldn't remember exactly, but she surely wasn't an ordinary Castilian woman—whose connection with this rough, some might say downright violent sport he was unable to determine. However, what the young woman was talking about seemed like magic to him, like something translucent and ethereal, yet in some intimate and not easily explainable way also crystal clear, in spite of the fact that he, strictly speaking, understood almost nothing. What is more, although he didn't realize at first why she decided to address that unusual chain of words to him of all people, he was certain that what she said had to do with the very essence of nothing other than boxing, Cuban boxing in particular. The girl brought up one abstract idea after another, none of which Unamuno was familiar with. What imprinted himself especially deeply in his memory was a surname that had just been mentioned, likewise unfamiliar to him, but he supposed it belonged to some obstinate Catalan (or Basque) heavyweight, some greenhorn who had yet to earn the title of a fighter.

As the conversation progressed, Unamuno was becoming more and more convinced that it was something that would change his outlook on boxing, and therefore on life itself. As he was sitting at that table of apparatchiks laden with beer bottles and overflowing ashtrays at the Olympic Village in Moscow in the summer of 1980, the Tragic Sense, *el sentimiento trágico de la vida*, revealed itself to him in all of its enlightening totality. He felt it in his chest, like a devastating explosion that flattens everything before it and sets off when you least expect it, like José "Mantequilla" Nápoles's left hook. It felt like satori. "Yes, life is tragic. It is purely and insufferably tragic from the moment we realize we're going to die someday; I knew that even before the lady so eloquently told me. But then I realized the only thing that matters. Namely, that a fighter dies twice or never. And, on the one hand, that doubled the tragedy, albeit on paper only, theoretically. On the other hand, it allowed for the possibility to avoid the tragedy altogether. I'm just sorry I didn't grasp that when I was still in the ring myself. When there was still hope that I'd throw a mean uppercut and dethrone death," he said, and lowered the paddles that were his palms.

With a convert's zeal he sermonized on holy individualism, the vector hissing like hot blood in the ears of every full-blooded fighter. Then, running his palm across the injury that cost him his career, he methodically presented the hypothesis that the entire history of Cuban boxing should be written anew as an *intrahistoria*—a cycle of common stories about common people, a fresco packed with amateurs from the dilapidated suburbs, curmudgeonly barmen and bouncers from the casinos in El Centro, and some other really abstract things, but the grandson and I had lost him long since. Cuba was pulsing around us like an underground radio station, a persistent signal transferred onto everything that breathes, and it makes all the flesh under the needle of the world vibrate like a distant, possibly long-extinguished star. We handed Unamuno a half-full bottle of Cristal and continued to descend to the ocean down Prado Street, as his untamable, titanic shadow blended with the raging night that had, in the meantime, soaked up almost everything.

Curvas Peligrosas

I

Awake in Cancún

I DREAMT THAT I promised someone, on my own deathbed, or by someone else's, that one day, when the rains subside and light clouds press down like verbs on the cryptic sentences of trees, I would by any and all means go to Cancún instead of Comala. The vow was given in a convulsion, and it was an immeasurable relief to see the moment when that intense, silent disquiet in the muscles—my own or someone else's—was swept away by the gentle silence of death. I do declare: all the days of one who has just departed this life wouldn't suffice to describe properly the horror of Cancún, the dead city. That expanse, that barren field of stupidity, glass, and dreams, waking dreams of being someone you're not, someone tanned, in Speedos, if only for a second. The vast, false expansiveness of that cold horror was drumming in my temples when I was shaken awake from my nightmare by an announcement addressed, beyond any doubt, to us, the crumpled passengers on the economy flight to Cancún. Although it was the middle of January, plumes of hot air rose from the sand and asphalt, obscuring the atmosphere, refracting the last sunrays of the day, making the scene unpleasantly pink. Down below the belly of the aircraft stretched hot, cramped beds of resorts, apartment blocks, massage and nail spas, and beach and rooftop bars intersected by vertical rows of windowed hotels, reflecting the boring sunset, prolonging and multiplying it infinitely, it seemed. I wanted a glass of water, but there wasn't one to be had. I wanted to fall back into that deathbed dream, immediately.

There, deep in the rear, where escape buses depart from, in the part of the city from which the ocean and all that it washes ashore seems indescribably alien, I stood leaning on the reception desk, talking to Inés. Before her, I knew only two women with that name. The first, who certainly had a Gypsy tint to her tan—something that in my earliest childhood stopped me by some incomprehensible magic from saying no to her—disappeared from my everyday life before I turned seven, after which I met her sporadically, only to forget her almost completely in the end. The second was, and remains, the Tenth Muse, the Mexican phoenix, a poet's word embodied in the featherlight, contagious body of Sor Juana Inés de la Cruz, the wondrous daughter of the Baroque, the Baroque in whose essence also lies something quite obviously Gypsy. Between me and the third Inés, a front-desk clerk at a motel that smelled of chloroform and bedbugs, lay the wakefulness of continents, one night that

MARKO POGAČAR

never happened, that chafes like a stone in your shoe but at the same time attracts you like a magnet. Camouflaged in the aroma of coffee and tacos, from the kitchen came the promise of a future, while the present, that which still hasn't been claimed by the rusty vise of the past, undeniably carried the sweaty, elusive smell of Inés.

The latter, my real Inés, could say little and nothing about most of these things. She'd never been to Comala, and had no desire to go. Not even after her relative Ramón got married there on Día de la Constitución two years ago. "He married stingy Comalan trash, as stingy as only Comalans can be. They have only heat, goats, and rocks in abundance," she says, and as far as she's concerned he would've done better to stay here, at the edge of Yucatán and the world, home with his mother. Noon was approaching; the sun in its zenith peeled the pale plaster off the walls, coat by coat, and the omnipresent, powerful, whiter and whiter light made the very thought of sleeping presumptuous. I bought a copy of *La Crónica de Hoy*, wiped the sweat off my forehead with a handkerchief, and half-whispered the last thing Inés said to me: "Forget that stupid Comala, they marry their cousins, they say people over there are prone to growing a tail because of that."

I boarded a red ADO bus to Tulum.

Eclipse in Tulum

SOME PLACES REEK of misfortune. Some misfortunes, however, quite certainly bear, like a brand in the skin, the distinct smell of the place, a smell that is almost visible. There are places whose blooming carcasses radiate the pulse of entertainment, a plague oppressing mankind by imitating that questionable quality known as life, demystified in medical textbooks, yet still elusive. Cities and towns, especially those whose night is tacked to the sky with studs arranged in the shape of the Southern Cross, are commonly given away by a blend of all those qualities in all possible combinations and ratios, some even temporally stratified, pointing to an unreal *before*, while the smell itself, with its strong, sleepless hands taps out, like an insane telegraphist, a quite certain *after*. Tulum, needless to say, was obviously one of those places.

A town in the state of Quintana Roo, one of the last ones abandoned, no sooner than they were built, by Mayas running from the burning sword of Juan Díaz of Seville, an evil white god tremulous from rum and gold. I arrived there for 170 pesos on the red bus in which they played canción ranchera. The soft, feathery, yet penetrating voice of Vicente Fernández Gómez, the king of ranchero music better known by his nickname Chente, issued forth from below his shoe-polish-black mustache, ricocheting off the portraits of saints pasted to the windshield, orbiting like a drunken pendulum around the Savior's nude body, which in turn orbited the rearview mirror in concentric circles, grazing the driver's spiky top slathered with grease, finally to nestle, like a lucky stray bullet, in the creaky station door. The door opened straight to Avenida Tulum, a street that looked like it had fallen out of a film about a much more colorful and really quite tame Wild West. I opened the newspaper and scanned it for weather—the small, bright-yellow sun, printed in bold, fully matched the one in the sky. The lunar calendar, however, showed a complete, irrevocable eclipse that night.

The Mayan city, on the edge of the modern-day one, a field of decaying palaces, indescribable houses, and temples with steps that once flowed with hot blood, was also dead, but in a different, more literal way. Yet, the wind still lived there in the crowns of the palm trees, and the nation of iguanas held court, calm as if they were sipping coffee in a cantina on Calle Mercurio or walking in the Dos Aguas park, in the heart of a story about a downfall. Bavarian tourists with sunburned backs were thumbing through pulp novels and dipping slices of green mango in salt. Megalithic stone

MARKO POGAČAR

blocks crumbled under the sun's sledgehammer into unexpected, quite Catholic dust. The temple of frescoes was behind my back as my eyes, blurred by an excess of light, were getting used to the excess of the ocean. I undressed, because it's better to be naked when you're close to death, and dove under the turquoise surface.

Down in the tranquil depths swam giant rays, colorful fish, and turtles hatched in my father's days, in happier times gentler on turtles and humans alike. In addition to the turns and pirouettes of the airborne Vaslav Nijinsky in *The Rite of Spring* or *The Afternoon of a Faun,* the gracious swaying of a ray was reminiscent of William Butler Yeats's slow, rolling lines peppered with some good old Luis de Góngora. "Among School Children" meets, and is sodomized by, the timeless *The Solitudes,* in a dark corner, possibly to death. In the subtext tremored a whiff of Angelus Silesius's mysticism. The turtles moved through the blue in a less terrifying manner, more akin to a slowly stumbling four-stroke engine. Their telegraphic lurching summoned the verses of the postal worker August Stramm, confronted with Vasko Popa's equally brief, albeit much more abstract descriptions of animals. I named each ray and turtle Pedro, for my long-sought father.

When I emerged, the evening was already there. Still alive, the yellow wheel of the moon illuminated the rot of Tulum, and was barked at by feral dogs. At a bar called Apelido I ordered a double Pelotón de la Muerte and a pint of warm Victoria, then almost immediately another mezcal and more Victoria. Quite obviously, the original night was rising up in the sky, the night in which the light loses its last tangible stronghold, a darkness that would certainly return someday, this time more heavily armed. The black shadow of the planet conquered inch by inch until there was nothing but a realist portrait of the future in an oval frame hanging in the middle of the Tulum sky like a coal apple. "If only there was an elevator to take us up there! The moon is a dance floor where clumsy, lost poets of Europe try to dance salsa!" declared Lotte, a Dutch woman with sea snail shells around her ankles, hopping in place to a techno beat. "Let's go!" she said without thinking, oblivious to the fact that the eclipse was becoming permanent, that every elevator, one way or the other, took you to the execution site in the end.

Palenque, Both Alive and Dead

ABOUT MYSELF I was able to say little and nothing, although I, quite understandably, had frequently encountered myself. All of that fit into one slim paragraph: I was a bearded, balding man about to turn thirty-five, a bit of a Greek nose, tall and hard of hearing, determined to write and uproot himself as thoroughly as possible, and—the following phrase is to be understood in completely and radically ideological terms—to leave his home and his element. I was wearing short jeans, sneakers whose uppers were bored into by toenails affected by an advanced case of athlete's foot, and a shirt made of a lighter shade of denim, studded with mother-of-pearl buttons, with sleeves I normally kept rolled up high, but I unrolled them, and took off my counterfeit Ray-Bans with too-dark lenses, as the deceptive Mexican night neared. I was a dandy and in thrall of a vice or a passion which we'd better not talk about at the moment. Stiff and sore from the twelve-hour bus ride and utterly devoid of any thought, that is how I arrived in Palenque.

It wasn't yet dawn, and the moon's watermark was still visible in the designated corner of the sky. Under a hospital neon light, the bus station kiosk employee poured an American portion of sugar into my Americano, as the few passengers curled up in the plastic chairs or sleepwalked with their eyes stuck to a digital display. The dream hadn't finished just yet; the waking hours hadn't quite started. "There," I said to myself, not really sure what *there* referred to. "There," I repeated into my chin, for I was one of those terrified, god-forsaken people, people who say *there* to themselves. An obese woman in a floral-pattern dress greedily licked the stamp, and with a look of indescribable disgust on her face handed the postcard over to the thick postal darkness.

"Seems like it'll never dawn here," she said. The final syllables still echoed in the lifeless hall as a tanned, tattooed hand effortlessly lifted an oversized backpack. "Let's go find some breakfast," she said, and that for a second seemed less hopeless than endless resignation, an ethos that had completely taken me over of late, compressed into that reticent *that* word. Ten minutes later, pushers of psychoactive mushrooms, posing as mariachi bands and Lotería Nacional sandwich men, distributed their merchandise as Palenque slowly woke up to soapy water in the beer gardens of early-opening bars, and dogs lazily stretched their limbs, hobbling toward the first bones of the day tossed to them. Like shadows, mustachioed men with large, melancholy eyes roamed the streets. We shared a portion of huevos rancheros, and Hannah, a waitress from Canada, decided, reassured by a cliché I uttered, to spill before me, over coffee and a few glasses of fresh-pressed juice, her entire New Brunswick life, all of its sweat and snow and tears, the sum of all tears wept on that cold continent.

Here, from these winding streets, these neatly trimmed tree crowns, one indescribable monument to the planet, and Hannah's soft sobs, starts the living Palenque and its death, its silent death anthem. There is no Hannah there, no thick mycelial madness, no place for a *there*. The jungle is strewn with pyramids, observatories for watching forgotten stars, thrones overgrown with weeds, temples of blood and time. A crystalline mountain river meanders through the scene carrying untranslatable words, sighs that sound as though they came from Remedios Varo's paintings, soaring from the mouths of Lola Cueto's dolls. It's all too big, too lost; it's all too dead. Yet, the accurate Mayan calendars still tick away in the background somewhere, like jungle clocks. Roots bite into the flesh of stone. And deranged flocks of sheep rush headlong down the catacombs, as if Indiana Jones were slowly sinking into deep sleep. I've named every sheep and every raven Pedro, after my father, who I must've been getting dangerously close to now. "There," I said into my chin, looking at a Predator figurine that from the profile looked like Donald Trump. "There," I repeated, when I reached the very top, when everything below me, as far as the eye could see, looked like it was on fire.

San Cristóbal de las Casas, Slowly Sinking

I ADVANCED SOUTHWARD. With Tabasco behind me and Guatemalan jungle to the left of my left kidney, I dripped down the map of Mexico with a vivid sense of descent that I always have when I'm going south, although I was actually ascending all the time. I felt like a renegade cursor on a synoptic chart forecasting the end of time; I shivered like the needle of a drug addict's compass. The bare highlands of Chiapas, gray and brown rocks, and groves of cactuses like battalions of massive, rampant penises stuck from the other side of the glass to the skin of my cheek pressed close to the window of a white van with *Bienvenidos a Tulum* written on the side. The whole region looked like an oversized pincushion, and I like a holey sock. The driver's bald crown bobbed before my eyes for hours like a will-o'-the-wisp. I named him Pedro, and abandoned myself to the vice of sleep.

The wind rolled empty cans and fresh cigarette butts across a dusty parking lot on the other side of Mirador; the sound of heels on fine gravel carried the scattered rhythm of shakers, and the squeal of tires took on the role of the first violin in a satanic salsa orchestra. For twenty pesos the taxi driver took me to a hostel in the district of 5 de Mayo, not to be mixed up with the eponymous, much more upscale street of colonial villas and lavish gardens. The consolation prize was the fact that spring had always been my favorite season, the time when nature awakens and bonfires are lit on the Feast of St. John, like in Gypsy songs or Wordsworth's and Amy Lowell's poems. All of that hardly protected me from the brisk night in the mountains. I put on everything I had and lay in the back till daybreak, counting the hundreds of speed bumps which the van, wriggling along the meandering roads through villages whose names I've forgotten, sent to an unknown Zapatista hell that night. I bade myself a good morning as soon as it dawned. "Mornin'," replied Paul readily, as if someone had sent him to my rescue.

Born in Berlin in 1946, he rose from a pile of rubble like a skinny phoenix suckling along with smoke that went up from the craters of allied bombs, five-ton steel sows with messages like "die, pigs" and "here you go, Krauts" scrawled on the slick steel. His mother never told him, she merely hinted once without looking him in the eye, but Paul was the result of the biggest mass rape campaign in the history of mankind, a consequence of one of several thousands of childbirths that marked, with a scream, a defeat and a broadly understood victory. He credited his father, a Russian soldier of unknown rank and origin, for his love of classical music and his proneness to a typically Slavic melancholia. He learned a hundred Russian words online, and he sometimes played the Soviet anthem on YouTube and cried soundlessly. I had to admit to myself that I, too, shed the occasional tear when I heard odes to a distant, long-lost freedom. At the same time, I had to talk Paul out of the idea he had for the two of us to sob Slavically together, here in this garden, for all eternity. Since 1948, after all, he had lived mostly in America—initially, for years, at a military base. The last seven years he'd been spending in a room in this same hostel on Calle Honduras, opposite the barbershop San Francisco and the First Emmanuel Church of the Nazarene, reading doorstops with onionskin pages left there by the visitors, and preparing to return to Nürnberg, home, to be closer to his multiplying relatives scattered across the German desert. I didn't know if he'd finally realize that there was nothing to return to, just like there was nothing to folk wisdom. The following night, before we parted, he hugged me, patted me on the shoulder and whispered in my ear счастливого пути, wishing me a safe trip and making sure I caught his weary smell.

At that moment the bloody sunset above San Cristóbal was already dimming out, like a young revolution slowly fading away. However, all that fades has got to have shined at least once, repeated Subcomandante Marcos, Delegado Cero, as he patrolled one of the nearby autonomous villages before bedtime. There, behind the silent forest of my ribs, a vast church that was sinking into ever-thicker darkness still watched over the town, a church whose interior was illuminated with neon and decorated with plastic flowers, the seat of a Black Jesus reminiscent of a Black transvestite prince. But no darkness is as dark as the darkness of the church. No theology is a liberation theology.

Oaxaca; or, On tiredness

"OHOHOHOHO," GUFFAWED PEDRO P., the driver of a red ADO bus that squealed when it braked, twisting with one hand a mustache resembling Emiliano Zapata's, only lightly holding the steering wheel with the other. "Ohohohoho," he repeated, somewhat more quietly this time, when the vehicle stopped dead in its tracks, as if petrified after a collision with Medusa's gaze, in front of four equally startled schoolgirls wrapped in short white-and-deep blue coats who'd just decided to cross the road. I thought to myself, without any particular reason: neon. It's the neon that devours icy darkness from the heavens; neon is the only thing that can save us. Then I continued, still silent, to update the catalogue of my dreams, trying hard, at all costs, to stay awake, at least till next nightfall.

The song "Dr. Psiquiatra" by Gloria Trevi spread from the glaring plasma TV in the corner—*bo bo bom*. Proper Mexican music, funny, intelligent, and, above all, passionate—*bobo-bobo bom bom bo bom*—miles above those epic, saccharine

Peruvian sagas about condors, or the feebleminded reggaeton ditties that shake the dance floors of the continent, from Puerto Rico to Tierra del Fuego. In spite of the catchy melodies and beats that set the hips on fire, eyelids, like blinds on store windows after closing time or bars on prison windows, rolled down inexorably over the dark windows of the soul.

In the seductive yet temporary darkness, a review of one-minute pieces played out on the fleeting screen of slow, heavy blinks, a film journal of sorts depicting the last two sleepless days. The first roll contained a seemingly endless ride across mountains, a slow tumble over highlands reminiscent of the moon's surface overgrown with cactuses resembling organ pipes and yucca trees that looked like burning bushes, with the idea of end, embodied in eagles and plump vultures, similar to death in *The Death of Artemio Cruz*, watching over everything. The second contained obscure nocturnal scenes. Police checkpoints, pat downs conducted by pimply lads with rifles, pissing at an indeterminate hour in the desert swept by a hot wind akin to the Alpine föhn that lifted storm clouds of dust. Sellers of turquoise sleeping bags, mosquitoes the size of a coin in noxious cantina toilets, the spitefulness of the wasteland as lavish as the sum of everything that is at the same time ongoing and has already come to pass in *Terra Nostra*, a victorious skull cramping, like in the accursed Leopoldo Méndez's illustrations. The third roll was quite abstract, as it dealt mostly with unimportant details from Mexico's

MARKO POGAČAR

bloody history—unpredictable yet fully expected deaths of men, roosters, snakes, dogs, and other animals that were evidently much less interesting in the filmmaker's eyes.

I checked in at a small, family-run hotel named Casa Carmen, or Casa Cristina, or, possibly, Casa Catarina, and unwrapped the still-hot tacos I'd bought at the taco shop opposite. The city pulsated everywhere around me like a heavy veal heart. Colonial cathedrals sprayed the Baroque of plague and smallpox around, torn posters advertised badly paid jobs in catering, salsa bars lured patrons with stage lights and the chatter of percussions, and the tattooed hipster waiters from expensive chocolateries slowly melted bars of pure cocoa. As night approached, the streets around the main square became louder and louder, and Plaza de Zócalo came to life properly. Like in a kaleidoscope the shape of a trumpet mute, a kaleidoscope inserted into the mouth of a trumpet of the Apocalypse, entertainers of all sorts scurried about on the cobblestones, fire caters and drunken jugglers, a shower of mariachi bands and elderly couples dancing salsa in the shadow of the chessboards, and above all of that, neon, endless neon in the sky reflected by the few low clouds.

¡Pa' todo mal...mezcal y pa' todo bien...tambien! stood above the bar at a small inn by Mercado La Cosecha, and I decided to take that as my motto; desiccate my wakefulness and pin it down like a rare insect to an upholstered corkboard. After a series of bars filled with similar patrons

with similar intentions, on my way home—to Casa Carmen or Cristina or, quite possibly, Catarina—I stumbled, as if upon a lost Comala, upon New Babylon. Sticky rumba was playing inside, in the semidarkness. Maricas on a date were cuddling over flickering candles, patrons were ordering cocktails with names like Oaxacan Slushy, Marrakesh Express and Mezcal Paloma, while a gringo, who looked like a man I hadn't seen in years, was putting his hands up the skirts of tipsy girls. A girl in a too-warm poncho, possibly tipsy herself, was writing lines and lines of neat text with a fountain pen, and watching over all of that from the doorframe were three melancholy poets drinking tepid Victorias, long-haired poets in dark denim, chubby although relatively young, out of whose back pockets and leather bags slung across the shoulder poked notebooks with crumpled pages; in short, three lost men who couldn't have been anything else but melancholy Mexican poets in the heart of a Saturday night lost in the vast archive of the world's wasted Saturdays, and I concluded that one could only love them. I lifted up my glass, and immediately lowered my forehead onto the dirty table.

Neon, only neon can save us, I thought and instantly forgot the whole thing. I only knew that everything was terrifying, and that only memory, the closest and most similar of all things in existence to a dream, could guarantee the words their meaning, the intangible secret reality from the attic of our night.

II

OUT OF NOWHERE, from the other side of the rusty fence of metal sheets welded together like a postcard from another world and another time, sounds of a string quartet rehearsing—a performance abruptly interrupted after a few minutes for a deep, acousmatic voice to issue an undismissible two-word warning to the viola; just like that, flat and without an exclamation mark, but with a streak of refined despair: *la viola*. The melody that immediately continues to spread through the invisible openings is a melancholy one, heavy and sweet, possibly glazed bitter on the edges, like a bandoneon piece by Astor Piazzolla, or a Carlos Gardel song rearranged for that autumn film by Bergman. All of it, the whole hovering sonic image, belongs to a narrow backstreet not far from the vegetable market in Oaxaca in the eponymous federal state, a few hours' drive away. Now, for no reason it seems, it rings in my inner ear as I descend the steps of the Morelos station, metro line B, steps that lead straight to the dusty heart of Colonia Morelos, a neighborhood "poor since Aztec times."

My delayed miniature for strings was promptly replaced by the roar of Avenida Congreso de la Unión, blended with hard hip-hop whose lyrics I couldn't follow. I carried hunger under my armpit, and days of accumulated fatigue that was plunged suddenly headfirst into the nightmarish flurry of Distrito Federal. Like everyone else, I carried the virus of death, seeking at the same time a layman's diagnosis, an antidote, and a shrine for it. I had waking dreams mostly, on my feet, because sleep meant loss of precious time which was sedimenting on forgotten, written-off calendars as if on a final hospital bed chart in which the entries stop abruptly and irrevocably.

The station square was filled with vendors of fruit, veg, and household items. Their stalls, on the other side of a tract of road graffitied with oversized, naive portraits of politicians, artists, and athletes, were engulfed by the deluge of the flea market, and all around, on cardboard boxes, plastic sheets, or the piss-stained asphalt between the stalls, sat, lay, or stuttered a multitude of the drunk, drugged, and deranged. It was six in the afternoon, and dusk was slowly curling up underboot; tremulous figures with faces shaded by visors and greasy hats shouted *¡Hola, gringo!* or rattled something incomprehensible. I didn't respond. With my eyes firmly fixed on the eyes of Nelson Mandela and then the eyes of wrestler Alejandro Muñoz Moreno, better known as Blue Demon, I bought four oranges and drummed on the fence of a red-brick residential complex,

MARKO POGAČAR

fortified with crushed glass and locks of barbed wire. In the corner of the front yard, an elderly lady was roasting beef offal. Colorful lights left there from Christmas switched on and off to the deadly, hysterical staccato of an orchestra only they could hear, stretched over a bed of equally colorful flowers that looked like tulips. From a slick-haired guy in a sleeveless undershirt in a knickknack store by the entrance steps I bought soap, a bottle of water, and beer, then I bolted the door with a ¡Viva AMLO! sticker in the green, white, and red of the Mexican flag behind me. The acronym for Andrés Manuel López Obrador flashed for a second like a vernal promise of a future. Down the avenue, alluringly, spoiling the plans of passersby and dogs, crawled the smell of burned flesh.

* * *

In daytime, when they're broken down by the penetrating whiteness of light, some things look different indeed, lighter, alive in their own way that was previously hidden by a patina of darkness and reduced to a rumor, as if the light with its well-known sorcery could translate a wholly fatalistic script into a much more optimistic film. The picture of misery remains, however, unchanged.

In the cacophony made up of noon bells, street vendors' hawking, roosters' crowing, and the hiccuppy traffic of Avenida del Trabajo, I dip churros into a cup of coffee, while all around me the typhoon of the Tepito market sweeps the ground. Everything that one such divine vacuum cleaner could pick up and then drop back down randomly to be sold is here, where the omnipotence paradox looks different: Can god buy something he decided isn't for sale? That despot who exists in the same way as the part in Donald Trump's hair exists, as an absence given away by a shower of supposed traces of its presence. Plastic rosaries swinging at eye level. Display counters with tacos glowing, blessed by Our Lady of the Neon. Under the stands, the mute dogs of Santería lie sleeping.

J. and I trudge along the hot roads, waiting for J. to finally join us. We kick cans and spit on the ground to feel the resistance of our own bodies; we try to leave the impression of tough yet laid-back guys. We choose the people whose eyes we'd meet, though we know we don't stand a chance. Streets perpendicular to Avenida del Trabajo look like neatly stretched white lines. Until you stick your nose in one of them, it's impossible to tell which one is flour, and which one hides a rat poison speedball. J. is a biochemist, and I myself have a penchant for chemical compounds; rather than into the hubbub of children kicking balls and the silence of the old men playing cards in the shade of Mexican cypresses, we turn into a street of nameless solvents, glue, crack, heroin, and cheap booze, in which morning looks like an eclipse at noon. We pretend it's none of our business. From a wall ready to be knocked down we read, syllable by syllable, a graffito about poetry, freedom, and sodomites (possibly a mistranslation), as two tattooed, proficient Spanish speakers (possibly the authors of the text at hand) get up from an air mattress and head toward us. One of the translators is named Jorge, as in Luis Borges, the other José, as in Lezama Lima. Although all the characters in this chapter, obviously, have the same initials, which opens up the space for a potentially interesting identity play, we opt for a conventional story and hurry home without waiting for the end of the verse, to check if J. is finally awake.

But there is no escaping death. Puffing, we turn the first corner, from where we can discern the solacing, spray-painted concrete of the line B. A mural with the masked face of Rodolfo Guzmán Huerta, who earned the nickname El Santo in close combat, grows in our eyes when our path is blocked by a massive glass sarcophagus, the altar and the home of Nuestra Señora de la Santa Muerte, Our Lady of the Holy Death. Candles, plastic flowers, paper lanterns, count-out rhymes, and icons inject new life into the brittle yellowness of the bone; the teeth of the veiled skull seem to be snarling: *rosebud, rosebud*. The veil is shaking from heavy footfalls. Pigeons shit on the glass. Quite strangely, unfathomably, no person living or dead—in this chapter, as in all of Comala—is named Pedro tonight.

* * *

J. and J. and I are sitting under the glowing sign of the hotel Hidalgo, on the outer rim of the gentle desert of boredom, peeling pumpkin seeds. The burning neon of letters intertwines and blends with the redness of the western sky, a reflection of a hundred-year-old revolution which, understood as an active principle, still smolders above the Porphyrian secession style of the Palacio de Correos and its dazzling, Escheresque staircases, as well as the winged dome of the Palacio de Bellas Artes. A saxophonist on the corner reminds one of a young Gerry Mulligan, or someone who has swallowed Mulligan who now blows from the bottom of a vast, dark belly, as if from a tomb or the body of a whale. The birds flocking above the dome bear an incredible resemblance to swallows.

I dreamt that J. was a character in Sam Peckinpah's *Bring Me the Head of Alfredo Garcia*, one that doesn't appear at all in the final cut or, for that matter, in the script itself. In my dream, J. was part of a conspiracy between a villain known as El Jefe and Terese, his daughter, while the head which, like John the Baptist's, was to appear bare on a silver platter was mine. There are dreams better and dreams worse than us, but most people, it seems, are forever imprisoned in their worst dream. Proust says we love only that which we do not possess completely, but the head resisted that appeasing logic: it insisted on remaining, as a precondition for that love, whole. This morning, upon waking, I was utterly unable to say with certainty which one of the two J.s it was.

I told them that as we moved from the seeds to boiled corn on the cob. The two of them couldn't agree which one would be better suited for the role, and they made a series of (mostly legitimate) objections, considering the context of Proust's thought and the way in which the dream was dreamt. By that time we were already going up Ignacio Allende Street toward Plaza Garibaldi, thinking about swapping elotes for pulque or beer. That night, Mexico truly seemed a land of metamorphoses.

At Plaza Garibaldi, some mariachi bands were striking up their corridos, while others, in preparation for making their own contribution to the general cacophony, tuned their instruments or lolled about under the trees, making sure not to soil or wrinkle their uniforms reminiscent of melodeons. Ice cream summarily melted in the hands of children; homeless people and alcoholics sprawled on greasy cardboard sheets along the edge of the square. J. and T. and I opened our cans of beer, hearing the familiar, soothing hiss, as if something were boiling in the belly of the can. A minute later, two special police officers, armed with tear gas and long guns, kindly offered to put us away for thirty-six hours, or skin us alive for drinking in public, pursuant to some insane fines list. We started negotiations. The officers—possibly Juan and Jesús—negotiated like the Sphinx: we looked, smelled, and above all spoke like a reliable European cajero automático. As I was taking a thick wad of pesos in the negotiated amount of about 90 US dollars to the backyard of the bar Salón Tenampa,

I was thinking about the head that was once Trotsky's. In the famous incident that took place in the summer of 1940, in a house with red walls a half-hour metro ride away, that head, owing to the perfidious political reaction and the pointy tip of an ice pick, unfortunately failed to remain whole. In the light of that thought, in a state similar to something that may be considered wakefulness, I now believe Proust was right.

We ran into a nameless bar to have the most expensive beer in our finite lives, thankful for the apparent absence of the Mexican legal system and law enforcement we found there. Victory seemed distant, the enemy untouchable, but we knew it couldn't be that way.

*   *   *

Two days later, at the pulquería Pakaly, in low voices melting into whispers, we planned a march on Coyoacán. In addition to the famous Blue House of the Kahlo/Rivera couple, there is the abovementioned Red House, where Stalin's swine Mercader, in one imprecise stroke, managed to open a sizeable hole in the nape of Leon Trotsky, while the blood that gushed forth from the opening at an incredible rate drew a quite abstract dark-cherry fluid map of the free world on the white tile floor. A young poet and door-to-door salesman, Roberto, was to be our guide, and we made detailed preparations by, among other things, thoroughly studying Rivera's murals in the garden of Palacio Nacional for hours on end. We paid special attention to the monumental *History of Mexico*, which, according to certain obscure interpretations of Trotskyist kabbalah, pointed to a slew of potential executioners, although it was completed five years before the incident. The list included a failed assassin, Iosif Grigulevich, Stalin's ambassador to Yugoslavia, who, due to the paranoia and plot twists of the Cold War, had also been tasked with killing Tito.

The walls of Pakaly were covered with framed photographs of Mexican wrestling heroes, first and foremost Blue Demon, El Santo, Mil Máscaras, and Gory Guerrero, and painted with the portraits of relatives—distant and close, animal and human—of Calavera Catrina, stepdaughter of the demonic engraver José Guadalupe Posada, as well as dozens of varicolored sugar skulls of all sizes. Fat drunks flashing ass cracks and punks with pierced noses lazily lifted their eyes when Roberto entered, impeccably dressed. R. is one of the younger members of the inner core of an organization known as Círculo de Poesia, which could be described, concisely and quite accurately, as a poetry cartel: a publishing house, a poetry festival, a literary magazine, as well as a distribution network— a department Roberto heads, hopping from one Mexican town or village to another in his van stickered with the cartel's logo. We popped by the José Martí Cultural Center to pick up some kind of a package, then spent an hour breaking through the horror of the traffic toward the former colonial satellite village long ago swallowed up by the hot animal of the city. Roberto talked about silence, about violence, and those other cartels, about the longest Mexican night whose bottom looks like the bottom of a bathtub where our lives now spin and twirl like a skein of belly-button lint. In his vocabulary, the name Andrés Manuel López Obrador stands for hope as of recently. Hope was in high demand, and back then was among the best-selling books in the country.

Not far from the central square, a square green and pleasantly, extravagantly restless, we ate pizza topped with cicadas and talked about words that weave the invisible yet omnipresent filling of the world, a mysterious stuffing that lends existence the taste of adventure and unpredictability, making it at once similar to a headless holiday turkey. This finely woven cloth is its cradle, its shirt, and its shroud, but, like in the fairy tale about the new clothes, the world emperor has in fact been naked before our eyes the whole time. When one catches it fortuitously, one ought to wring its neck immediately, lest it slip, slick and greasy, out of one's hands, like a wrestler wriggles out of a clinch, or a pig about to be stuck unexpectedly outwits its slaughterer. In codes broken long ago, we talk about Benedetti, Vallejo, Paz when it can't be avoided, about fences and masks, about the cold, distant planet Pizarnik. We sit in expectation of something—anything—to happen, in silent pursuit of an event, something that could metastasize into a literary text. At last we realize our mistake. Late-afternoon light lands

on the terror of the happening, and this mild, soft illumi-
nation becomes its devastating Termidor: the only relevant
and absolutely necessary happening in a literary text is the
happening of literature itself. We sit, till from the darkest
depths of our own night, a night that *is* us, an indescribable
choir bursts into a cicada death song.

* * *

"Santiago de Chile is the most boring city in the Americas! At
least in Latin America. At least for me. But what's the use of
entertainment for others, entertainment that meets other
people's criteria that must be awful?" says Renata, as we
swallow Peruvian ceviche and octopus of unknown origins
in a restaurant not far from the hipster bar Bósforo. "It's
dangerous over in Guatemala—the moment the sun goes
down, I put a blow-up doll on the passenger seat to fool the
highway robbers," she says. "It's dangerous, but at least you
don't die of damn boredom. My kingdom for a good rob-
bery—provided, of course, you get robbed by some interesting people—I sometimes catch myself thinking," she
says, before ordering another round of drinks. I've heard
similar stories about the streets of Guatemala City from my
poet friend Francisco Nájera, a wild professor who started
his career as a manual laborer in the Bronx in the first half
of the sixties, after he'd left those streets behind for a while.
He spoke a bit of English, a bit of Spanish, in an impeccably

flowing linguistic fugue, as the shadow of a washed-out city grew before my eyes. This story, however, is neither about Chile, nor is it about Guatemala, although it's impossible to separate it from these two places.

I met Renata for the first time over ten thousand kilometers from here, at a time when she worked for an unusual, semisecret agency, the purpose of which I never understood completely. Now she works in education in some other boring, faraway city where she lives, although this could be a cover. I was thinking about that after we'd moved to Bósforo, an elongated place with a single toilet, lit by dim, gambling-room light that was spreading from low-hanging lamps like lazy fog. In that intrepid cloud, just as in all of Mexico, for that matter, the patrons seemed at the same time alive and thoroughly dead. I suddenly thought it was quite possible that somehow I'd managed, unknowingly, with my eyes shut and my heart open, to reach Comala.

I was startled out of this sweet fantasy by the sound of a familiar language. It sprayed around the narrow room in a polyphony, which now didn't seem like a fugue but rather an organum lost in the darkness of the world, whose soft yet discernible cantus firmus was made up of the whispers of a choir of slaughtered chickens. Seven people at the adjacent table from all over Yugoslavia, from Niš to Metković to Drniš, came to celebrate a friend's marriage and visit the Aztec empire. After all, are our customs, our kingdoms, our churches and wars, our arsons and human sacrifices one iota different

MARKO POGAČAR

from the Aztec ones, whose cruelty, inscribed in stone, we
seek in order to feel the silent shivers of fear and be at the
same time anointed by a sweet mise en abyme of progress?
That's what I was thinking about as we were having round
after round of tequila and mezcal, spirits that don't substan-
tially differ from rakia. After all, the same agave trees that
bear the fruits whose fermented pulp the holy fiery water is
distilled from grow on the slopes of Vis, an island barely discernible on the map though larger than itself, an island that
swelled up in my memory like an inflamed liver, an island
where I'd met Renata for the second time.

Then we walked aimlessly down the streets of Colonia
Doctores for days, waiting for something to happen under the
boarded-up windows and unplastered walls, something that
would wound but not kill us; down the streets of the northern
and southern part of Colonia Roma, its villas, past their prime,
blossomed again, filled with beautiful people and new money,
immersed into the tidy yet unbridled green of the long boule-
vards; down the slow streets of La Condesa, which flowed—
in lasting memory of countess María Magdalena Dávalos de
Bracamontes y Orozco—in parallel with our lives carrying a
fallacious seed of sorrow, a seed that, quite possibly, could've
been gutted with a straight razor and burned around the next
corner. Making our way through the rivers of the undead in
a slow slalom, for days we refused to notice a rock I'd been
stumbling on the whole time, a rock hewn into a monument,
opened into the heavy, windproof pages of a book.

So I stood in front of that book, thin in its paper form, but here, in stone, as thick as a Bible, only much bigger, of course, for that was a book about the real, about life and death at the same time, about the here and the now, the then, and the who knows when, in one and the same perishable body, godless flesh above which night was falling forever. I stood before that cross-eyed Pedro Páramo reduced to a promise and planted near Avenida Hidalgo, as if I were a monument to something myself, thinking about a house that didn't exist, about a faraway home that disappeared and returned unexpectedly, like the clatter of a freight train. I felt all of Mexico pulsing around me like a huge, dried-out comma, wondering if anything here could ever birth a full stop.

MARKO POGAČAR was born in 1984 in Split, Yugoslavia. He has published fourteen books of poetry, fiction, and nonfiction, for which he has been awarded numerous Croatian and international awards. In 2014, he edited the *Young Croatian Lyric* anthology, followed by *The Edge of a Page: New Poetry in Croatia* (2019). He has received fellowships, grants and stipends from organizations such as Civitella Ranieri, Récollets-Paris, Brandenburger Tor, Passa Porta, and DAAD Berliner Künstlerprogramm. His work has been translated into over thirty languages. His poetry collection, *Dead Letter Office* (2020), was a finalist for the National Translation Award.

MIRZA PURIĆ is a literary translator from German, BCS, and Slovene, most recently of Faruk Šehić's *Under Pressure* (Istros Books, 2019) and, in cotranslation with Ellen Elias-Bursać, of Miljenko Jergović's *Inshallah, Madonna, Inshallah* (forthcoming, Archipelago Books). His work has appeared in *AGNI*, *Asymptote*, *EuropeNow*, Lit Hub, and elsewhere. He is a contributing editor at *EuropeNow*, and has served as an editor-at-large at *Asymptote*.

About Sandorf Passage

SANDORF PASSAGE publishes work that creates a prismatic perspective on what it means to live in a globalized world. It is a home to writing inspired by both conflict zones and the dangers of complacency. All Sandorf Passage titles share in common how the biggest and most important ideas are best explored in the most personal and intimate of spaces.